My

New Mexico

Journal

Pambling Roads

Books by Pamela Ackerson

The Wilderness Time Travel Series
Across the Wilderness
Into the Wilderness
Wilderness Bound
Warriors of the Wilderness
Out of the Wilderness
The Wilderness Series Ebook box set

Wounded Heroes Anthology (with Debra Parmley, Teri Riggs, Maggie Adams, and Nia Farrell)

PI Series Time Travel
The Gingerbread House
Garrett's Ghost
Living the Wright Life

Historical Fiction
Dear Margaret,

Non-fiction
I Was Just a Radioman (A memoir of a Pearl Harbor survivor, Black Cat, and decorated veteran.)
Be More Successful with Marketing and AdvertiZING
I am a Runner — the Memoirs of a Sepsis Survivor

A Granny Pants Story   (Children's Stories)
The Long and Little Doggie
Riley Gets into Predicaments
Available in Spanish:
El Perrito Largo y el Perrito Pequeno (La Serie del Perrito Largo y Pequeno)

Short Stories

The Clere Restaurant Collection
Sunday at 7
With a Side of Love
Winds from the Past
The Throuple with Love
The Best Catch of His Life

A Rosa for Russell ~ from the Wounded Heroes Anthology

Pambling Roads Journals —

Pages for you to fill in the blanks! Nurture your creativity with Pambling Roads State Journals, interactive journals designed to spark imagination and self-motivation. They include historical trivia and tidbits about each state, and a small section in the front of the book by the author sharing her travels.

States:

Alabama   Arizona   Arkansas   California   Colorado   Florida Georgia   Idaho   Illinois   Indiana   Iowa   Kansas   Kentucky Louisiana   Maine   Maryland   Massachusetts   Michigan Minnesota   Mississippi   Missouri   Montana   Nebraska Nevada   New Hampshire   Rhode Island   South Carolina Ohio   Oklahoma   Tennessee   Texas   Virginia   Washington, D.C.

More to come! Check your favorite bookstore for the latest state journals.

Fortune Cookie Wisdom Journals

My New Mexico Journal
Pambling Roads
Pamela Ackerson

© Pamela Ackerson 2020

Cover Design: Dora Gonzalez

PamelaAckerson.com
@PamAckerson
Pam@PamelaAckerson.com

Our travels have brought us all around the "lower 48". We've tried to zip zag, circle through, and around every state we could. Florida was where this endeavor started.

Enjoy your journal.

Thank you for taking this wonderful journey with us. It has been absolutely incredible.

Please keep in mind that some museums don't allow photography and will not be available on the Pambling Roads Blog

Pambling Roads—My New Mexico Journal

New Mexico

Welcome back to Pambling Roads, where we are documenting our travels in the United States (and Canada) to "Meet the Americans".

We were expecting to meet people from all over North America. It has been a wonderful adventure of a lifetime. We have met people from all over the world.

Gallup

We stopped for the night at the LaQuinta on small section of Route 66. We only stayed at the Gallup hotel for one night. It was a comfortable stay and the employees were polite and friendly. Whenever we make any kind of stop-over, we always drive around and check out the area.

Farmington

On our way to four corners we saw Ship Rock from a distance. Actually, you couldn't miss it. The rock rises over 1900 feet about the land and over 1600 feet wide. It stands tall among the landscape and the closer you get the more it looks like a ship. The dikes trailing behind the rock look like waves created from the ship.

Four Corners

The only place in the United States where four states connect together, Arizona, New Mexico, Colorado, and Utah. A granite and brass marker is used to show the exact connection of the four states. We took pictures standing in all four states and walked around the area and can now say we were in four states in the same day, in the same hour.

There were Native American booths where everyone could enjoy the different crafts, jewelry, and food.

Salmon Ruins

We ran out of time for the day and were planning on visiting Salmon Ruins but they had already closed. It was recommended as a great place to go.

We were going to head to Santa Fe, but one of the couples we had met had just came from there and said they were having a lot of trouble with hotel robberies and stuff. So we decided that perhaps we will return another time and explore Santa Fe.

Socorro

We stayed at the Best Western in Socorro, as expected, they excelled in their service. We stopped by the Socorro Visitor's Center. My husband said hello to the lady in the office. She did not respond to him. I asked if perhaps she had not heard him and he said she did because she was looking straight at him when he said hello. She never came out of her office to see if we had any questions or needed any help.

We looked around for pamphlets and information so we could see what we would like to explore in Socorro. We drove around looking at some of the older homes until we reach the church.

The San Miguel Mission Catholic Church

We got a small glimpse of the inside of the mission. The church is one of the oldest catholic churches in the United

States. It was being worked on and we could not go inside. We did stop by the museum and gift shop. The ladies there were very nice. One of them was a volunteer and she had suggested that we go to the wildlife refuge and gave us directions.

Bosque del Apache National Wildlife Refuge

We spent a few hours thoroughly enjoying this well maintained wildlife refuge. They told us about the rare bird that was spotted and had never been seen before in the U.S. We went to a few spots hoping to be one of the rare handful of people to spot the rufous-necked wood rail bird. We did not spot it, but did see quite a bit of wildlife.

They have a visitor center/gift shop and the employees there were very friendly and passionate about their jobs. They were very happy to answer our many questions.

White Sands Missile Range

We didn't know that the site was only open twice a year. We were a bit disappointed but the guard at the entrance was quite pleasant and understanding. He told us about trinitite, a rock created from the blast. He suggested that we stop at the store in Bingham, a very small town, where there is a rock shop that sells the trinitite.

The Trinity Test Site

Blanchard Rock Shop in Bingham NM

We were hoping to purchase some trinitite. The store was closed so we continued on with our trip.

The Valley of Fires

The Valley of the Fires recreation area is an area that had a volcanic eruption about 5000 years ago. We walked around some of the lava flow pits and sections. It was amazing how far this lava flow had gone. Going into the Valley of Fires Park we realized how vast it really was.

There is camping and trails which we enjoyed thoroughly. The view was spectacular.

The visitor center was closed for lunch so we were not able to get inside and see what they had on display in their exhibits.

We drove around Roswell… so cool.

Carlsbad

Living Desert Zoo and Gardens

We arrived in the late morning to a wonderful surprise. They were holding a mineral and gem show. We walked around a bit, checking out the vendors before we went back to the desk to purchase entrance into the zoo and gardens. The garden specializes in native plants of New Mexico and the Chihuahuan Desert. It's a beautiful walk through sand hills and desert uplands.

As you walk about, you will view an aviary with several types of birds including a bald eagle, golden eagle, and roadrunner. There is a nocturnal and reptile exhibit. You will see Bison, Pronghorn, Mule Deer Elk, a cougar, bobcat and several other animals that are native to the area.

All the parks' personnel were wonderful, pleasant, and welcoming. We spoke for a while with the gift shop ladies. They greeted us as we entered the room and were pleasant to visit with as well. One of the ladies was familiar with Florida and we chatted about the hurricanes and the differences between New Mexico weather and Florida weather.

Carlsbad Caverns and Carlsbad National Park

Absolutely fascinating. Wear a jacket, it gets a bit chilly down there. If you have any physical issues either be prepared to be hurting, take the elevator, or pass on the harder tours. Don't forget to stop at all the pullouts, you will miss a lot of fascinating geological sites if you skip them. Bring water so you can stay hydrated while you are outside walking some of the trails.

Lincoln National Park

Sitting Bull Falls and Recreation Area

WOW! Right smack in the middle of a desert the 150-foot waterfall gracefully falls to pools of cool water. This is a movie-worthy mirage moment that is real. It is a beautiful oasis with green plants and cool water for swimming. There are places to sit under natural curved rock for shade. Standing near the falls, one can just feel the power and beauty of the earth.

There are trails that can be hiked, picnic tables, pavilions, fresh water, and bathroom facilities at the park.

The turquoise is the state gem.

The greater roadrunner is the state bird.

The black bear is the state animal.

The yucca is state flower.

The state tree is the pinon pine.

The state motto is *Crescit eundo* which means, it grows as it goes.

Some arrowheads found in New Mexico have dated back to over 10 thousand years old.

Gallup is the 'Native American Capital of the World'.

Some of the buildings in Taos Pueblo are over 900 years old.

Moon rocks are at the International Space Hall of Fame in
Alamogordo.

At 7000 feet above sea level, Santa Fe is the highest capital city in the United States.

White Sands National Monument is a desert created by white
gypsum crystals.

The Navajo reservation covers 14 million acres.

Most of New Mexico's lakes are man-made.

Albuquerque hosts the world's largest international hot air balloon festival.

Hatch is the 'Green Chili Capital of the World'.

The Elephant Butte Reservoir is the state's largest lake.

Grants produced the most uranium in the United States.

There are more cattle than people in New Mexico.

The first atomic bomb was tested at the White Sands Missile
Range.

St. Paul's in Las Cruces has seven bell choirs.

Deming has annual duck races.

New Mexico's nickname is Land of Enchantment.

Angel Fire is home to the annual Shovel Race Championship.

The Bandera Ice Cave is one of the oldest caves in the area.

New Mexico has an extraordinary amount of UFO sightings.

Now a ghost town, Elizabethtown was the first town in New Mexico.

75% of the roads in New Mexico are not paved.

Roswell has an International UFO Museum and Research Center.

In Taos, there are multi-storied adobe homes, some more than
1000 years old.

In 1536, the Spanish arrived, leaving the area with rumors of the Seven Cities of Cibola.

Built in 1610, San Miguel Mission is the oldest church in New Mexico.

Santa Fe, the oldest capital in the U.S. was founded in 1610.

Built in 1610, the Palace of Governors is one of the oldest public buildings in the U.S.

In 1610, Gaspar de Villagra published the first print book about the New World.

____

____

____

____

____

____

____

____

____

____

____

____

____

____

____

____

____

____

____

In 1610, Gaspar de Villagra published the first print book about the New World.

In 1626, the Spanish Inquisition was established in New Mexico.

In 1706, Albuquerque was founded.

In 1821, Mexico declared its independence from Spain.

Gold was found in the Ortiz Mountains in 1828.

In 1863, the Long Walk began, relocating Navajos and Apaches to Bosque Redondo.

Roswell, known for its UFO encounters, was founded in 1869.

In 1878, the railroads arrived in New Mexico.

Built in 1880, Hotel la Fonda del Taos is the oldest hotel in New Mexico.

In 1898, Thomas Edison filmed the first movie in New Mexico—Indian Day School.

Founded in 1899. Santa Fe High School is the oldest school in New Mexico.

In 1923, oil is found on the Navajo Reservation.

Los Alamos National Laboratory was established in 1943, and is one of the foremost research institutions in the United States.

1945 marked the testing of the atomic bombs at Trinity Site.

In 1947, a rancher found unusual debris from a crash in his pasture in Roswell.

In 1948, Native Americans are given the right to vote in state elections.

Smokey the Bear was a real bear. He was found alive in a tree after a forest fire in Lincoln National Forest in 1950.

In 1950, Uranium is discovered near Grants.

The Aztec Ruins National Monument has preserved structures built by the Pueblo Indians.

Las Vegas, New Mexico is the oldest film location for movies in the United States.

____

____

____

____

____

____

____

____

____

____

____

____

____

____

____

____

____

____

With a population of 56, Folsom Village is the smallest town in
New Mexico.

Rumors and legends say there are haunting among the halls of the Fort Stanton Historic Site.

Located east of Ruidoso Downs, Fox Cave has a gift shop inside the cave.

There's a Turquoise Museum in downtown Albuquerque.

The world's largest Chile pepper is in Las Cruces.

Organ has a Space Murals Museum.

Roswell has an Area 51 Museum.

Smokey the Bear Historical Park is located in Capitan.

In Deming, there's a Bataan Death March Monument.

Chaparral has the World's Largest Firecracker.

Santa Rosa has a Route 66 Automobile Museum.

Carlsbad Caverns has over 10,000 bats.

The El Rancho Hotel in Gallup was a popular place for the movie stars to stay.

The National Solar Observatory is located in Sunspot.

Socorro is also known as the other UFO landing site.

There is an old Aztec Mill Museum in Cimarron.

Places of Note:

Shiprock ~~
Geoinfo.nmt.edu/tour/landmarks/shiprock/home.html

Four Corners ~~
Navajonationparks.org/htm/fourcorners.htm

Salmon Ruins ~~ SalmonRuins.com

San Miguel ~~ MissionSanMiguel.org

Bosque del Apache National Wildlife Refuge ~~
FWS.gov/Refuge/Bosque_del_Apache

Trinity Site ~~
WSMR.Army.Mil/PAO/Trinity/Pages/default.aspx

Valley of Fires ~~
Blm.gov/nm/st/en/prog/recreation/Roswell/Valley_of_Fires
.html

Roswell ~~ SeeRoswell.com

Lincoln National Park ~~ FS.usda.gov/Lincoln

Thank you for purchasing your wonderful journal so you could fill in the blanks.

It's been a great adventure for, meeting the Americans, and meeting people from all over the world. Don't forget to check out the other Pambling Road Journals.

They make wonderful gifts.

Have you been to any of the places I've mentioned? Do you have stories to tell as well? Visit the Pambling Roads Blogs and add in your comments.

PamelaAckerson.com
Twitter: @PamAckerson